How To Become *Spiritual* Without Being Religious

KEN REINERS

AuthorHouse™
1663 Liberty Drive
Bloomington, IN 47403
www.authorhouse.com
Phone: 1-800-839-8640

© 2013 by Ken Reiners. All rights reserved.

No part of this book may be reproduced, stored in a retrieval system, or transmitted by any means without the written permission of the author.

Published by AuthorHouse   01/16/2013

ISBN: 978-1-4772-9452-9 (sc)
ISBN: 978-1-4772-9451-2 (hc)
ISBN: 978-1-4772-9453-6 (e)

Library of Congress Control Number: 2012922352

Any people depicted in stock imagery provided by Thinkstock are models, and such images are being used for illustrative purposes only.
Certain stock imagery © Thinkstock.

This book is printed on acid-free paper.

Because of the dynamic nature of the Internet, any web addresses or links contained in this book may have changed since publication and may no longer be valid. The views expressed in this work are solely those of the author and do not necessarily reflect the views of the publisher, and the publisher hereby disclaims any responsibility for them.

Other books by Ken Reiners:

THERE'S MORE TO LIFE THAN PUMPKINS, DRUGS AND OTHER FALSE GODS
ADDICTED TO THE ADDICT: From Codependency To Recovery

Ken Reiners is an ordained United Methodist Clergyman and a Licensed Marriage and Family Therapist. He has had sixty-six years in a wide range of experiences in the secular and religious world. He has been in the parish ministry for twenty-two years and a Hospital chaplain for twenty-five years. Ken was a spiritual care counselor for eighteen years to chemically dependent youth and adults in an inpatient treatment center in Minneapolis, MN. His spiritual counseling includes a ministry with run-away youth in a half-way house, criminally disturbed youth on a locked mental health unit and a motorcycle gang called the "Dayton Outlaws." Ken has appeared on the Phil Donahue, television talk show and the P.M. Magazine Special. He has given lectures to patients and their families at Fairview University Hospital and many workshops to schools and churches in the Mid-West, sharing his family's journey of recovery from the disease of chemical dependency. Ken is married, has two married children and four grandsons.

To my brother, Virgil, a Vietnam Veteran,
who died far too young in the service of his country.

To Ian McNicholes, my Kinship friend,
who elicits my inhibited playful child.

ACKNOWLEDGEMENTS

I am indebted to my wife, Helene, for her love and support throughout our marriage. She is my best friend. She has always been a positive influence in my life. Her loving and caring attitude has not only influenced me and our children but many of her business associates and friends. Her success in the business world as a Senior Executive National Sales Director, has brought her fulfillment and happiness which has enriched our marriage. Helene has said that she has a PHT degree (Put Hubby Through), meaning she put me through four years of college, three years of divinity school and three years of graduate school as the main bread winner. Helene's success, as a business woman, has also helped pay for our four grandson's education and allowed us to travel world-wide.

I thank my good friends, Eric and Mary Jo Hruska, for their willingness to read my manuscript and provide valuable feedback for enhancing my book including the necessary correction of my errors.

I am particularly grateful for all my spiritual mentors who have enlightened me on my spiritual journey. They are, my loving friend, Dr. Grant Tanner, my clinical supervisor, Dr. William A. Miller, my pastor, Rev. Mark Miller, Roman Catholic priests: Fr. William Kenney, Fr. George Coyan, Fr. Steve LeCanne; my best friend, Helene, to name a few.

CONTENTS

Acknowledgements xi
Introduction xvii

1. Spirituality And Religion 1
    1. How spirituality is different from religion.
    2. Spirituality defined.
    3. God has many names.
    4. Eight spiritual needs for human growth.

2. Seeking a Relationship With a Higher Power 7
    1. We seek a power greater than ourselves.
    2. Our idea of God is learned from our parents.
    3. Letting go of our parent's God.
    4. Need to develop our personal religion.

3. Living a Positive Philosophy of Life 17
    1. The value of positive thinking.
    2. Accurate optimism vs. feel good optimism.
    3. Three dimensions of accurate optimism.
    4. Letting go of pessimism.

4. Overcoming Shame 25
    1. Shame is toxic to our being.
    2. Shame is confused with guilt.
    3. Guilt vs. Shame.
    4. Characteristics of Adults Shamed in Childhood.

5. Renewing Moments of Transcendence 31
   1. Our need for peak experiences.
   2. Peak and plateau experiences defined.
   3. Examples of peak and plateau experiences.
   4. Moments of transcendence lead to happiness.

6. Having Congruent Values 37
   1. What happened to our values?
   2. Values are essential to spiritual wholeness.
   3. Violation of values leads to spiritual illness.
   4. Guilt can bring conformity to our values.

7. Trusting and Being Trusted 41
   1. Elephant in the living room.
   2. Taking the risk of being hurt again.
   3. The power of forgiveness.
   4. Trust is earned.

8. Joining Caring And Nurturing Communities 45
   1. Spiritual growth occurs in caring communities.
   2. Isolation leads to spiritual death.
   3. Examples of healing from caring communities.
   4. Wisdom comes from disappointment.

9. Developing Our Higher Self 51
   1. Soul is Higher Self.
   2. Higher self defined.
   3. Pain can build character.
   4. Examples of developing higher self.

Appendixes 55
   A. A Letter From an Atheist 55
   B. Never Good Enough: The Legacy Of Shame 59
   C. A Letter to my Father 65
   D. Garden Song—John Denver 69
   E. Animals as Spiritual Guides by Ken Reiners 71
   F. Actions You Can Take In Working Through Your Shame 77

References 79

We are not human beings
going through a temporary spiritual experience.
We are spiritual beings
going through a temporary human experience.

—Pierre Teilhard de Chardin

INTRODUCTION

As I grow older I find myself growing less religious and more spiritual. I confess there are times I prefer to visit, as my brother-in-law used to say, "St. Mattress Church with Rev. Pillow preaching." There have been times I slept in on Sunday mornings rather than attend worship and I did so without guilt.

I used to tell my friends, somewhat facetiously, that I revised one of my favorite hymns changing it from "I was sinking deep in sin, far from the peaceful shore." to "I was sinking deep in sin, whoopee!" I discovered that many of the sins my fundamentalist religion taught me I shouldn't do-like dancing, playing cards, attending movies on Sunday, or drinking alcohol-are really fun. I felt like the little boy who prayed: "Lord, if You can't make me a better boy, don't worry about it. I'm having a real good time."

Many Christians continue to believe that sin is *plural* and the list is lengthy including the ones I listed above. Sin, in the Biblical definition, is singular and means "alienation" or "going against the will of God."[1] I sin by violating God's will and, therefore, alienate myself from God. When I'm asked by those who don't know I'm a clergyman, "Why do you wear a cross?" I reply, "Because I sin a lot and I need a reminder that I'm forgiven." The Bible says we are all sinners, therefore, we need forgiveness.

Episcopal priest, Robert Farrar Capon, wrote that "the church should not be in the morals business, manufacturing elaborate codes, rules and laws for living. Instead, the church's business is forgiveness."

We don't need moralistic judgments imposed on us by self-righteous people.

When I was attending Divinity School in Dayton, Ohio, I initiated a street ministry to the Dayton Outlaws in the bars, the jail cells and the court rooms. They were a motorcycle gang who severed their relationship from the Hells Angels Club because they wanted to run a "cleaner" club.

Three of the club members and myself were invited to be on the Phil Donahue, television talk show. During the show viewers called in claiming to be "Christians." They told me that I should "go to hell along with the Dayton Outlaws" for even associating with such "terrible sinners." A week after the show I received several hate letters from some more Christians telling me where to go.

Far too often some organized religions or churches have been shaming and judgmental rather than loving and caring. This moralistic, judgmental attitude and other personal reasons has made religion offensive to many. In 1999, Dr. David Elkins, a licensed psychologist, wrote in "Psychology Today":

> Studies show that most Americans want spirituality, but perhaps not in *religious* form. Researcher Wade Clark Roof, Ph.D. from the University of California at Santa Barbara, found that in the 1960s and 1970s baby boomers dropped out of organized religion in large numbers: 84% of Jews, 69% of mainline Protestants, 61% of conservative Protestants and 67% of Catholics. Many left the church and synagogue not because they had lost interest in spirituality, but because organized religion was not meeting their spiritual needs.[2]

A recent study, by the Pew Forum on Religion and Public Life, reported that the number of non-believers in America was 15.3% in 2007, and has leapt to 19.3 % in 2012. Pew reported that "The group called 'Nones' is now the nation's second largest category after Catholics and outnumbers the top Protestant denomination, the Southern Baptist." However, of the 17,010 respondents, the study concluded that even though the non-believers have risen in numbers since 1970, "they're still interested in spirituality."[3]

How To Become Spiritual Without Being Religious

Let me clarify. I am not discounting religion or religious beliefs. There are some churches and synagogues that are meeting the spiritual needs of their members. I attend a United Methodist Church in Coon Rapids, Minnesota, and it is contributing to my spiritual needs.

My point is that certain religious beliefs or organized religion can be hazardous to one's religion *and* spirituality. There are radical religions today spewing a sick theology that believe it's God's will to kill the infidel. If religion does not enrich one's spirituality then it has lost its way. Spiritual growth happens when we can discard the distorted theology and myths imposed upon us by others.

Scott Peck, an American psychiatrist, best-selling author and best known for his book, The Road Less Traveled, said that the psychiatric profession owes its very life to the church. Why? Because, he concludes, most people who have great emotional difficulties come from religious homes where God was portrayed more by a minus sign rather than a plus sign. It seemed that God was always out to get you. "Don't do this or you'll be sorry!" "Live in fear because God sees every mistake you make."[4] Sound familiar?

Peck tells of Kathy, who wanted to die, because the torment of an all-seeing and all punishing God ripped the very life out of her waking hours.[5] He tells of Theodore, who entered his office an atheist, because he couldn't stomach the God of his parents: always looking down in judgment; always waiting to strike. Theodore became a minister because he finally asked the deepest questions of his soul. When he did, he found God didn't hate him for it.[6]

When I say I'm growing less religious and more spiritual, I mean that I am discarding the religious baggage that stunted my spiritual growth for years. I am letting go of the distorted religious theology that made me a prisoner of my soul. There has been a new found freedom in my spirituality.

For those of you who are atheist, I want to say a few words about my use of God language in the following chapters. When I speak of God, I am referring to what Alcoholic Anonymous calls a Higher Power or God as we understand him. If that's still offensive you might think of God as Giver Of Direction. What are some givers of direction that can help you grow spiritually? Maybe it's an AA sponsor, a pastor, close friend, teacher, or Al-Anon. Another means might be to add an "o" to the word god and you have "good." What is the greatest good for your spiritual growth? You might ask yourself, for example, "Is giving up drugs the greatest good for my spiritual growth?", or "Will having an AA sponsor be the greatest good for my spiritual growth?" (See Appendix A: "A Letter From an Atheist").

A stereotype image of God prevalent in the Judeo/Christian faith is that God looks like an old man with a long, white beard and hair. This is a failed attempt by man to define God in human terms. A. H. Maslow, a 20th century psychologist, who was best known for creating a theory of self actualization wrote:

> Even the word "god" is being defined by many theologians today in such a way as to exclude the conception of a person with a form, a voice, a beard, etc. If God gets to be defined as 'Being itself,' or 'the integrating principle in the universe,' or as 'the whole of everything,' or as 'the meaningfulness of the cosmos,' or some other non-personal way, then what will atheists be fighting against.[7]

There are no adequate words that can fully describe or define God. What is more important is to think in terms of how we experience the care of a power greater than we are. I experience the care of a Higher Power, for example, through people who accept me and love me without conditions, and who can help me grow spiritually.

The underlying reason for writing this book is my passion to create a spiritual, growth book that was simple to understand and provides the essential, spiritual needs for anyone seeking spiritual wholeness.

Specifically, this book can be helpful for individuals struggling with addiction problems, ranging from chemical addiction to sexual compulsivity. Furthermore, there are tens of millions family members related to these dependent individuals who are suffering from the addict's disease.

Finally, this book will be helpful for those who are interested in spirituality but have found that some organized religions or churches are not meeting their spiritual needs or are wanting to discard the religious baggage imposed on them by others.

The greatest disease in the West . . . today is not TB or leprosy; it is being unwanted, unloved, and uncared for . . . the poverty in the West . . . is not only a poverty of loneliness but also of spirituality.

Mother Teresa, <u>A Simple Path</u>

∴ 1 ∵

SPIRITUALITY AND RELIGION

What is spirituality and how is it different from religion? For the majority of people, spirituality is synonymous with religion. But it's not! On the other hand, there have been attempts to distinguish one from the other. Someone said that "religion is for people who fear going to hell and spirituality is for people who have gone through hell." Some definitions on the Web simply define spiritual as "clergy." or "income owned by the church."

All the above definitions are inadequate and exclusive. One difference between religion and spirituality is that religion is primarily external and spirituality is internal. Religion is a set of beliefs and doctrine that leads one to do something like praying, worshiping, fasting, serving, reading the Bible, whereas spirituality is something experienced internally like serenity, inner peace, love, compassion.

The Bible tells in James 2: 23-27:

> If any think they are religious, and do not bridle their tongues but deceive their hearts, their religion is worthless. Religion that is pure and undefiled before God, the Father, is this: to care for orphans and widows in their distress, and to keep to oneself unstained by the world.

In other words, our acts of worship, fasting, praying, should lead us to serving others. We <u>enter</u> the church or synagogue to worship and we <u>leave</u> to serve those who are needy in our world.

Religion can be both internal and external but that is not usually the end result, according to Maslow. He wrote:

> I see in the history of many organized religions a tendency to develop two extreme wings: the 'mystical' and individual on one hand, and legalistic and organizational on the other. Most people lose or forget the subjectively religious experience, and redefine Religion as a set of habits, behaviors, dogmas, forms, which at the extreme becomes entirely legalistic and bureaucratic, conventional, empty and in the truest meaning of the word, anti-religious. The mystic experience, the illumination the great awakening, along with the charismatic seer who started the whole thing are forgotten, lost or transformed into their opposites. Organized Religion, the churches, finally may become the major enemies of the religious experience and the religious experiencer.[1]

What is this *mystical* characteristic of religion that Maslow describes as "the illumination, the great awakening along with the charismatic seer who started the whole thing." I believe it is just one of many pathways to spirituality.

The word spirituality comes from the Latin root *spiritus* which means "breath," referring to the breath of life. Spirit, in the Bible also means "breath" or "wind". According to Dr. David Elkins, Professor Emeritus of Psychology in the Graduate School of Education and Psychology at Pepperdine University, spirituality,

> . . . involves opening our hearts and cultivating our capacity to experience awe, reverence and gratitude. It is the ability to see the sacred in the ordinary, to feel the poignancy of life, to know the passion of existence and give ourselves over to that which is greater than

ourselves. Its aim: to bring about compassion. Its effect: good physical and mental health.[2]

Kenneth Pargament, professor at Bowling Green University, defined spirituality as "the search for the sacred and at the heart of the sacred lies God, divine beings or a transcendent reality".[3] Borrowing from Pargament, Elkins and Alcoholics Anonymous, my definition of spirituality is, "the search for the sacred or meaning in life, and at the heart of the sacred is God or a power greater than ourselves. Its aim: to bring about compassion. Its effect: good physical, mental and spiritual health."

God has many names like Allah, the Muslim name for God; Higher Power, from Alcoholics Anonymous; Great Spirit from the Native American religion; Elohim, Yahweh or Adonai from the Hebrew culture or <u>G</u>iver <u>o</u>f <u>D</u>irection as I suggested in the introduction of this book. The list goes on and on. For the sake of keeping it simple I will be using Higher Power, in most instances, throughout the remainder of this book. With this in mind let us examine further the meaning of spirituality.

Albert Camus, was a French journalist, novelist and playwright. He won the 1957 Nobel prize for literature. He professed to be an agnostic and he once said, "To lose one's life is no great matter but what's intolerable is to see one's life being drained of meaning to be told there's no room for existing. A man cannot live without some reason for living." In other words, everyone is in search for the sacred or meaning in life and if you haven't found a reason for living you will die spiritually and/or physically.

Peck said, "Life is difficult." He quotes Buddha who taught that the first of the 'Four Noble Truths' is, "Life is suffering."[4] We can conclude from that truth we can find meaning even in our suffering. Nietzsche, an atheist and nineteenth century German philosopher said, "He who has a *why* to live can bear almost any *how*." In other words, whoever has a reason for living can bear almost any suffering.

The above premise is the thesis for Dr. Viktor Frankl's book, <u>Mans Search For Meaning</u>.[5] Dr Frankl, a Jewish psychiatrist, was a long-time prisoner in a German concentration camp. His father, mother, brother and his wife died in the concentration camps or were sent to the gas ovens. Only he and his sister survived to tell their stories.

Dr. Frankl discovered in the camps that those who had a will to live were the ones who survived while those "who saw no more sense in his life, no aim, no purpose and, therefore, no point in carrying on" were the ones who soon died regardless of how healthy they were.

He reported that the death rate in camp the week between Christmas, 1944, and New Years, 1945, increased. Why? Because the majority of the prisoners who had lived in the naive hope that they would be home by Christmas, gave up hope and died when it didn't happen.[6]

Our search for the sacred or meaning then, is vital to our survival. This is the answer to how we find meaning in a meaningless situation or any suffering. It is found in a Higher Power. Carl Jung, a Swiss psychologist and psychiatrist, who founded analytical psychology, alleged that spirituality was such an essential ingredient in psychological health that he could heal only those middle-age people who embraced a spiritual or religious perspective toward life.

Howard Clinebell, who was a United Methodist minister and professor at Claremont School of Theology, said that "Spiritual growth is the key to all human growth. There is no way to fulfill oneself except in relationship to the larger, spiritual reality."[7] He identified seven essential spiritual needs and they are as follows:

> *a viable philosophy of life . . . a relationship with a loving God . . . renewing moments of transcendence . . . creative values . . . developing our higher self . . . a trustful belonging in the universe . . . a caring community that nurtures spiritual growth.*[8]

In addition to the above seven spiritual needs I have added an eighth—"Overcoming Shame." The above spiritual needs, are the basis for becoming more spiritual. I hope this book will both challenge and encourage you to grow more spiritual.

One of the most spiritual things you can do is embrace your humanity. Connect with those around you today. Say, 'I love you', 'I'm sorry', I appreciate you', 'I'm proud of you', whatever you're feeling.

Steve Maraboli—<u>Life, The Truth, and Being Free</u>

~ 2 ~
SEEKING A RELATIONSHIP WITH A HIGHER POWER

There seems to be a universal drive in everyone that leads us to seek a power greater than ourselves. John Powell, Roman Catholic priest and professor at Loyola University in Chicago, wrote:

> All of us are willing to admit pangs of hunger and feelings of emptiness inside us. We experience half-formed dreams and vague drives for something more than human resources can promise or produce. There is in each of us a dynamic, a mystique or drive that, unless detoured by human selfishness leads us in search of God, whether we know it or not . . . It is a hunger that can be satisfied in God alone. [1]

St. Augustine, an early church father said, "Our hearts are restless until they rest in thee, O God." George Orwell, an English novelist and journalist, professed to be an atheist but he was confident that belief in heaven and hell helped keep us from being completely selfish and shortsighted. He was "obsessed with the need to find some substitute for that dying belief," according to David Lebedoff, and he concludes that Mr. Orwell "knew that we must believe in something greater than ourselves." [2]

What is vital to a healthy spirituality? It is our seeking out a caring Higher Power. Unfortunately, many of us grew up with an authoritarian or critical God. Psychology tells us that our idea of God is formulated in the first years of our lives. Scott Peck wrote:

> . . . when we are children our parents are godlike figures to our child's eye, and the way they do things seems the way they must be done throughout the universe. Our first (and, sadly, often our only) notion of God's nature is a simple extrapolation of our parents natures, a simple blending of the characters of our mothers and fathers or their substitutes. If we have loving, forgiving parents, we are likely to believe in a loving and forgiving God . . . If our parents were harsh and punitive, we are likely to mature with a concept of a harsh and punitive monster God. [3]

In the Christian faith the first prayer I was taught as a child was, "Our Father, who art in heaven . . ." I grew up with a father who ruled with a cocked fist and if I said or did the wrong thing in his eyes I was punished. The result was that my image of God was one who ruled with a cocked fist and if I stepped out of line I would be punished.

To this very day, I have negative feelings whenever I see or hear of the Upper Room, a daily, Christian, devotional book my parents read after the evening meal. If I snickered or whispered to one of my siblings during the devotional reading my father would slap me across the head repeatedly.

When we attended worship, during the testimonial time, my father would stand up and give a gushing testimony of what a great Christian he was. However, when we were going home, if I fought with one of my siblings he would slap me across the head even when he was driving the car. Again, not just once, but repeatedly.

Every Sunday I went to church I heard hell-fire and brimstone preachers tell me if I was not born again, I would burn in the fiery pits of hell. I went to tent, revival meetings where I heard the same negative and scary messages. As the evangelist closed his message, he would have an altar call inviting people to come to the altar and "accept Jesus Christ as your Savior because you might die when you go to bed tonight and wake up in hell tomorrow." My parents used the same argument to keep me in line when I failed to obey them or did something wrong. They tried to scare the hell out of me.

Someone said, "Hell is myself and other people." I believe there is a grain of truth in those words. Pogo, the famed, comic strip character said, "We has found the enemy and they is us." We can be our own worst enemy through self-abuse and violating our values. But hell can be other people through their abusive behavior of others, whether it be mental, physical, sexual or religious abuse.

One of my favorite fairy tales, is the story of Rapunzel. It is the story of a young girl who is imprisoned in a tower with an old witch. She is an ugly creature. Rapunzel is a beautiful child but the witch insists she is ugly like her.

Every day the witch screamed at Rapunzel: "Rapunzel, you're an ugly thing! You're just as ugly as I am!" The only person around Rapunzel is the witch. So Rapunzel believed her.

Now, it's the strategy of the witch to keep Rapunzel in the tower. If she believes she's as ugly as the witch she will never want to go out. People would be frightened of her if they saw how ugly she looked. Therefore, she stayed in the tower because the witch kept telling her she's ugly. At this point the story gets a little bizarre and my recall is vague.

One day, Rapunzel looked out of her tower window and she saw her prince charming. She looked down and he looked up and he saw how beautiful she was. And you guessed it. It was love at first sight.

Rapunzel has beautiful, long, golden hair and throws it out the window. Her prince charming is apparently a boy scout because he braids her hair into a ladder and climbs into the window. And when their faces are opposite each other Rapunzel sees, in the glistening part of his eye, that she's not ugly—that she's really beautiful. And then they parachute out the window or something and live happily ever after with a few minor incidents.

The illustration of the fairy tale is good for this reason: If somebody loves you in the glistening part of their eye, you see a reflection of yourself! You see a reflection of your beauty, your goodness. Our lives are shaped by those who love us and those who refuse to love us.

I no longer believe I'm ugly and neither do I believe in that "monster God" my parents instilled in me. My Higher Power is caring and loves me just as I am with no conditions. How did I come to that conviction? My first encounter with a loving God came through another father, my father-in-law. Bill was a big man with a big heart. He had a great sense of humor, love for life and people. He was not judgmental nor did he discount me. He loved me and accepted me just as I am.

Lillian Roth, a singer, dancer and entertainer became an alcoholic. In her book, "I'll Cry Tomorrow", she described how she recovered from her illness. She related the dark nightmares of many lost week-ends spent in the fog of alcohol. And she described the powerful grip that alcohol had on her and the many attempts to quit. Near the end of the book she spoke of her recovery and asked herself, "How was I able to do this?" She answered it simply but accurately, "I found someone who loved me and accepted me just as I am." [4]

I experienced that kind of love through my father-in-law, Bill. I was not consciously aware that his love for me was the catalyst that changed my concept of a monster God into a loving God. That awareness became an "aha" moment during my religious studies at college and divinity school. I began to discard my childish beliefs and developed my own belief system.

Peck wrote:

> There is no such thing as a good hand-me-down religion. To be vital, to be the best of which we are capable, our religion must be a wholly personal one, forged entirely through the fire of our questioning and doubting in the crucible of our own experience of reality . . . So for mental health and spiritual growth we must develop our own personal religion and not rely on that of our parents. [5]

My search for a loving God was forged through the fire of my questioning and doubting my parent's hand-me-down religion. However, not everyone seeks a Higher Power through questions and doubt. Sometimes God will pursue the non-believer Father John Powell, wrote about a student in his Theology of Faith class, who came to believe in a Higher Power because God sought him out:

How To Become Spiritual Without Being Religious

Some twelve years ago, I stood watching my university student's file into the classroom for our first session in the Theology of Faith. That was the day I first saw Tommy. My eyes and my mind both blinked. He was combing his long flaxen hair, which hung six inches below his shoulders.

It was the first time I had ever seen a boy with hair that long. I guess it was just coming into fashion then. I know in my mind that it isn't what's on your head but what's in it that counts; but on that day I was unprepared and my emotions flipped. I immediately filed Tommy under "S" for strange—very strange.

Tommy turned out to be the "atheist in residence" in my Theology of Faith course. He constantly objected to, smirked at, or whined about the possibility of an unconditionally, loving Father/God. We lived in class with each other in relative peace for one semester, although I admit he was for me at times a serious pain in the back pew.

When he came up at the end of the course to turn in his final exam, he asked in a cynical tone, "Do you think I'll ever find God?" I decided instantly on a little shock therapy. "No!" I said very emphatically. "Oh," he responded, "I thought that was the product you were pushing."

I let him get five steps from the classroom door and then called out, "Tommy! I don't think you'll ever find Him, but I am absolutely certain that He will find you!" He shrugged a little and left my class and my life. I felt slightly disappointed at the thought that he had missed my clever line—He will find you! At least I thought it was clever.

Later I heard that Tommy had graduated, and I was duly grateful. Then a sad report came. I heard that Tommy had terminal cancer. Before I could search him out, he came to see me. When he walked into my office, his body was very badly wasted and the long hair had all fallen out as a result of his chemotherapy.

But his eye were bright and his voice was firm, for the first time, I believe. "Tommy, I've thought about you so often; I hear you are sick," I blurted out. "Oh, yes, very, sick. I have cancer in both lungs. It's a matter of weeks."

"Can you talk about it, Tom?" I asked. "Sure, what would you like to know?" he replied. "What's it like to be only twenty-four and dying?" "Well it could be worse." "Like what?" "Well, like being fifty and having no values or ideals, like being fifty and thinking that booze, seducing women and making money are the biggies in life." I began to look through my mental file cabinet under "S" where I had filed Tommy as strange. (It seems as though everybody I try to reject by classification, God sends back into my life to educate me.)

"But what I really came to see you about," Tom said, "is something you said to me on the last day of class."(He remembered!) He continued, "I asked you if you thought I would ever find God and you said, "No!" which surprised me. Then you said, "But He will find you." "I thought about that a lot, even though my search for God was hardly intense at that time." (My clever line. He thought about that a lot!)

"But when the doctors removed a lump from my groin and told me that it was malignant, that's when I got serious about locating God. And when the malignancy spread into my vital organs, I really began banging bloody fists against the bronze doors of heaven. But God did not come out. In fact, nothing happened. Did you ever try anything for a long time with great effort and with no success? You get psychologically glutted, fed up with trying. And then you quit. Well, one day I woke up, and instead of throwing a few more futile appeals over that high brick wall to a God who may be or may not be there I just quit.

I decided that I didn't really, care about God, about an afterlife, or anything like that. I decided to spend what time I had left doing something more profitable. I thought about you and your class and I remembered something else you had said: 'The essential sadness is to go through life without loving. But it would be almost equally sad to go through life and leave this world without ever telling those you loved that you had loved them.'

"So I began with the hardest one, my Dad. He was reading the newspaper when I approached him. "Dad." "Yes, what?" he asked without lowering the newspaper. "Dad, I would like to talk with you." "Well, talk." "I mean it's really important." The newspaper came down three slow inches. "What is it?"

"Dad, I love you, I just wanted you to know that." Tom smiled at me and said it with obvious satisfaction, as though he felt a warm and secret joy flowing inside of him. "The newspaper fluttered to the floor. Then my father did two things I could never remember him ever doing before. He cried and he hugged me. We talked all night, even though he had to go to work the next morning. It felt so good to be close to my father, to see his tears, to feel his hug, to hear him say that he loved me.

It was easier with my mother and little brother. They cried with me, too, and we hugged each other, and started saying real nice things we had been keeping secret for many years. I was only sorry about one thing—that I had waited so long. Here I was, just beginning to open up to all the people I had actually been close to. Then, one day I turned around and God was there. He didn't come to me when I pleaded with Him. I guess I was like an animal trainer holding out a hoop 'C'mon, jump through. C'mon, I'll give you three days . . . three weeks.'

Apparently God does things in His own way and at His own hour. But the important thing is that He was there. He found me! You were right. He found me even after I stopped looking for Him."

"Tommy," I practically gasped, "I think you are saying something very important and much more universal than you realize. To me, at least, you are saying the surest way to find God is not to make Him a private possession, a problem solver, or an instant consolation in time of need, but rather by opening to love. You know, the Apostle John said that. He said: 'God is love, and anyone who lives in love is living with God and God is living in him.'

"Tom, could I ask you a favor? You know, when I had you in class you were a real pain. But (laughingly) you can make it all up to me now. Would you come into my present Theology of Faith course and tell them what you have just told me? If I told the same thing it wouldn't be half as effective as if you were to tell it."

"Oooh. I was ready for you, but I don't know if I'm ready for your class."

"Tom, think about it. If and when you are ready, give me a call." In a few days Tom called, said he was ready for the class, that he wanted to do that for God and for me. So we scheduled a date.

However, he never made it. He had another appointment, far more important than the one with me and my class. Of course, his life was not really ended by his death, only changed. He made the great step from faith into vision. He found a life far more beautiful that the eye of man has ever seen or the ear of man has ever heard or the mind of man has ever imagined.

Before he died, we talked one last time. "I'm not going to make it to your class," he said. "I know, Tom."

"Will you tell them for me? Will you . . . tell the whole world for me?"

"I will, Tom, I'll tell them. I'll do my best.".

It is a true story and is not enhanced.[6]

We can experience a loving Higher Power through many different means, however, there's none more powerful than through unconditional love like Tom experienced. My personal belief about a Higher Power came not only from my doubt and questioning my parent's hand-me-down religion but also from the unconditional love I experienced from my father-in-law. I no longer feel overwhelmed and burdened with shame. My spirit has been freed from the punitive, monster God imposed on me by my parents and religious leaders.

Being positive or negative are habits of thought that have a very strong influence on life.

Author unknown

~ 3 ~

LIVING A POSITIVE PHILOSOPHY OF LIFE

The freeing of my spirit from a punitive, monster God has enabled me to live a more positive philosophy of life which is essential to a healthy spirituality. In recent years, studies have revealed that a positive philosophy of life can have health benefits. Research studies have found, for example, that people who suffer from depression are at higher risk for heart disease and other illnesses.

Researchers at the University of Pittsburgh found that optimistic women live longer. In an ongoing government study of more than 100,000 women over the age of 50, the team found that eight years into the study, optimistic women were 14% more likely to be alive than their pessimistic peers.[1]

One of the most innovative and credible research studies on optimism was completed by Dr. Martin Seligman and his colleagues from the University of Pennsylvania, called the Penn Depression Prevention Project.[2] Dr. Seligman, a professor and renowned psychologist, has been studying depression for three decades. In his study of children and depression, his research proved that teaching children to challenge their pessimistic thoughts can prevent them from getting depressed.

The tools developed in the long term, research study taught children of all ages, life skills that transformed helplessness into mastery and bolstered genuine self-esteem. In addition, children who learned the skills of optimism, not only reduced the risk of depression but increased school performance improved physical health and provided themselves with the self reliance they needed as they approached the teen-age years and adulthood.

It is essential to understand the differences between the popular, feel good optimism and what Seligman defines as "accurate optimism." He wrote:

> The common sense view is that optimism is seeing the glass half full or always seeing the silver lining, or habitually expecting a Hollywood ending to real troubles. The positive thinking angle on optimism tells that optimism consists of repeating boosterish phrases to ourselves, like 'Everyday in every way, I'm getting better and better' to visualizing the ball dropping into the cup when we putt.[3]

Seligman's definition of "accurate optimism" is much more profound and elaborate than seeing the glass half full or always seeing the silver lining in every cloud of suffering.

He concluded:

> With twenty years of research, investigators have come to understand what is fundamental to optimism. The basis of optimism does not lie in positive phrases or images of victory, but in the way you think about *causes*. Each of us has habits of thinking about causes, a personality trait I call 'explanatory style.' Explanatory style develops in childhood and, without explicit intervention, is lifelong. There are three crucial dimensions that your child always uses to explain why any particular good or bad event happens to him: *permanence, pervasiveness* and *personalization*.[4]

Dr. Seligman gives excellent examples of each of the above three dimensions. An example of *permanence* would be the pessimistic child saying, "Tony hates me and will never hang out with me again." Whereas the optimistic child would say, "Tony is mad at me today and won't hang out with me." [5] "Children who are most at risk," Seligman says, "believe the causes of the bad events that happen to them are permanent . . ." but "children who bounce back well from setbacks and resist depression believe that the causes of bad events are temporary."[6]

An example of *pervasiveness* would be the pessimistic child saying, "Teachers are unfair." But the optimistic child would be more specific and would say, "Mrs. Carmine is unfair." Seligman explained that "Children who latch on to global explanations for their failures give up on everything when they fail in just one realm. Children who believe specific explanations may become helpless in that one realm, yet march stalwartly on in the rest." [7]

The third dimension of explanatory style is *personal* or deciding who is at fault. "When bad things happen, children can blame themselves (internal) or they can blame other people or circumstances (external)."[8] The pessimistic child might say, "I got a C on the test because I'm stupid." On the other hand, the optimistic child might say, "I got a C on the test because I didn't study hard enough." [9]

"Pessimism is a theory of reality," according to Dr. Seligman. "We learn pessimism," he concluded, "from our parents, teachers, coaches and they in turn recycle it to their children." [10] I would add to that list, religion and the military. I indicated earlier that I grew up in a negative family system and I can identify with the three dimensions that a child uses to explain why any particular good or bad event happens to him.

My negative conditioning from my father was instilled in me often by his abusive and punitive behavior. Whenever he lost a tool he would blame me for losing it. There were times, after verbally cussing me out for losing his wrench, he would discover later he had been sitting on it. I cannot remember him apologizing to me afterward. I learned from my father to blame others rather than blame a particular person.

I remember when I was in the fifth grade, for example, I tried to blame two eighth grade boys for some negative behavior that I did. Our country school house had a coal furnace in the basement and the first floor had a large, floor register where the heat came through to warm the one-room school house.

The teacher was in the basement shoveling coal in the furnace and the two older boys tempted me to throw an M80 firecracker down the furnace register. Of course, they just happened to have a firecracker on them. I yielded to temptation so I lit the firecracker and threw it down the register. Now, this was a powerful firecracker and when it exploded the teacher thought the furnace had blown up. After gaining her composure she figured out what had happened and she made everyone stay after school hours until someone admitted to the prank.

Shamefully, I admitted I was the culprit but I blamed the eighth grade boys and said, "They made me do it!" The teacher didn't buy it and held me accountable. My consequence was to stay after school every night for a week and write on the blackboard over one hundred times, "I will never throw a firecracker down the furnace register again."

I had lunch with a priest friend where I worked and every time after he finished with his main course he would go back to the buffet line and grab one of the delicious desserts. When he came back to the table he would say, "The best way to overcome temptation is to yield to it." Sometimes, like my firecracker experience, yielding to temptation does not always reward you with a delicious dessert. However, I did learn a lesson from the experience i.e. not to always yield to temptation because there may be harmful consequences.

I not only blamed others for my inappropriate behavior I was also good at blaming myself for the unacceptable behavior of others. I was twenty five when our son was born on May 4, 1961. He was four months old when I started college in the fall. I was a work-a-holic and I would spend most of my time in the classroom or studying at night. I was an absent father for both of our children. I attended Divinity School for three years after four years of college so I spent very little time with our children during those seven years.

Our son became a drug addict when he was seventeen and our daughter when she was fifteen. I told myself that it was my fault that they became alcoholics and drug addicts. I reasoned that our children's behavior must be related to the fact that I was an absent father. I shamed myself in thinking I should have spent more time with them when they were growing up. But after a week of family therapy I was told it wasn't my fault that our children became drug addicts. I learned in Al Anon that I didn't cause their addiction, I can't cure their illness and I can't control them but I did contribute to their addiction.

Seligman wrote, "Most often the general self-blamer believes that the problem is an unchangeable flaw in his own character." This prohibits the person from trying harder "to change the behavior so that he can prevent the problem or overcome the setback."[11]

Permanence is another conditioning I learned in childhood. I grew up under unrealistic expectations. No matter how hard I worked on the farm to win my father's approval, I could never live up to his expectations. If I plowed forty acres in one day, for example, he would be upset because I had not done more. If I got stuck with the tractor he would explode and scream, "You stupid s.o.b!!"

My unhealthy religion reinforced my negativity from the Sunday morning "hellfire and brimstone" sermons. Preachers told me what a "wretch" I was and if I wasn't "born again" I would burn in a "fiery hell" when I died. My confirmation taught me that I was evil and I had to prove myself worthy of God's love. I didn't hear about Creation theology until I learned in Divinity School that I was created in God's image and God created me *good*.

Once again, Seligman said, "The pessimistic child thinks about bad events as coming from abiding flaws in his personality, whereas the optimistic child thinks about moods and other temporary, changeable states."[12] I had a low self-esteem far into my adult years and I rejected any compliments I received because I didn't think I was worthy of them. I judged my *being* rather than my *behavior* and therefore, became helpless.

I had a fierce, verbal fight with my father when I turned eighteen so I left home and volunteered for the Army draft. I thought I was freeing myself from an abusive father but I found out rather quickly, I had only exchanged one negative environment for another. Basic training in the military was verbally abusive and if I didn't measure up to the high expectations I was punished. I received even more negative reinforcement of my personality.

However, by joining the Army I did free myself from a negative, toxic religion. I became an agnostic—maybe there's a God, maybe not. I didn't do it without suffering shame. My childish theology taught me to fear burning in hell for not attending church and denying the existence of God. This still haunted my conscience.

On the other hand it led me in search of a more positive and meaningful faith. When I was discharged from the military, I started reading the Bible again in search of the sacred or meaning. However, I was haunted by another religious incident I experienced when I was fourteen years old. I attended a Church Bible Camp where I made a commitment to full time Christian ministry. This experience led me to college where I began my studies for the ministry.

A course in Philosophy of Religion forced me to painfully challenge my simple, childish beliefs. There were times I left the classroom in tears, because I feared giving up those beliefs even though they were negative ones. I studied further and replaced those beliefs my parents had instilled in me with positive beliefs. My search for meaning led me to discover a positive philosophy of life that I'm living today. I am continuing to develop and grow in my spirituality.

A sense of shame is one of the most toxic emotions we can experience. Modern medical understanding of addictions and compulsivity tells us that our drivenness is often an effort to escape from or compensate for a profound sense of shame and inadequacy.

Dr. Robert Hemfelt and Dr. Richard Fowler
<u>Serenity: A Companion for Twelve Step Recovery</u>

∽ 4 ∾

Overcoming Shame

The negative conditioning I received from my parents, teachers, coaches, religious teachers and military personnel not only caused me to become a pessimistic person but was reinforced by shame. Shame had such a powerful and weighty impact on my spirituality that it continues to haunt me this very day.

Most of us have come out of shame-based, family systems and yet, shame is such an obscure and confusing concept that people find it difficult to differentiate between shame and guilt. I believe it is essential to understand the difference between the two in order to have a healthy spirituality.

It is easy to understand why guilt and shame are confused since they both involve feeling uncomfortable or bad. The distinction however, is that guilt is feeling uncomfortable with one's *behavior* while shame is feeling bad about one's *being*. Following are some distinctions between these two concepts:

Guilt is a violation of my values. Guilt is beneficial when the feeling forces me to reclaim my value of honesty again. When I was eight years old my older brother and I were playing with matches in the barn. We were lighting little piles of straw on fire so we could light the pretend cigarettes we made from weeds. Unfortunately, the fire got out of hand and burned down the barn.

When my father came home he asked me if I had any matches in my pocket. I told him, "No!" I had already ditched the matches but it was only a half-truth. I lived with that guilt of not telling the whole truth for ten years because I had violated my value of honesty. I was in the Army when the guilt weighed so heavily on me that I came home on furlough and admitted to my mother that I had burned down the barn. My mother said, "Your father and I were suspicious of you but we couldn't prove it." My telling the truth lifted a heavy load from my shoulders.

If guilt is a violation of my values shame is someone imposing their rules or values on me. Shame is when my parents told me I would burn in "the fiery pits of hell" if I went dancing. My parents believed that dancing was the "devil's game" which was based on the false indoctrination that they had learned from their fundamentalist religion. My failure to meet my father's unrealistic expectations of me was further cause for shame.

Guilt is a feeling that controls my behavior based on my values whereas shame is another person's attempt to manipulate my behavior based on their values. If I violated one of my parent's rules they would say, "Shame on you!" and I would be punished by a slap on my head or a spanking.

Guilt leads to acceptance of myself because I'm living within my value system. Shame leads to rejection of myself and lowers my self-esteem. "You're a bad boy" my parent's would tell me if I broke one of their rules. I spent many counseling sessions working to rid my life of shame and raising my self-esteem.

When I was in Clinical training I presented such a negative view of myself that my supervisor said, "Reiners, let me demonstrate how you present yourself to others!" He walked out of the room and came in walking backwards, bent over with his butt showing first. I was embarrassed and felt shamed because he did this in front of my peers. However, it was a graphic image that led me to rebuilding my self-esteem. This was probably one of the few times that shame was productive rather than destructive.

Shame is a pervasive, painful feeling that I have not measured up to someone's expectations and that I'm bad, worthless and inadequate. Shame is a harsh, critical judgment of myself that results in feeling unworthy as a person. The pain of shame can lead to a myriad of problems. In her book, *Shame & Guilt: Masters of Disguise*, Jane Middleton—Moz, Director of Middleton Institute and an internationally known speaker, listed 21 Characteristics of Adults Shamed in Childhood." They are as follows:

1. Adults shamed as children are afraid of vulnerability and fear exposure of self.
2. Adults shamed as children may suffer extreme shyness, embarrassment and feeling of being inferior to others. They don't believe they *make* mistakes. Instead they believe they *are* mistakes.
3. Adults shamed as children fear intimacy and tend to avoid real commitment in relationships. These adults frequently express the feeling that one foot is out of the door, prepared to run.
4. Adults shamed as children may appear either grandiose and self centered or seem selfless.
5. Adults shamed as children feel that, 'No matter what I do, it won't make a difference; I am and always will be worthless and unlovable.'
6. Adults shamed as children frequently feel defensive when even minimum or negative feedback is given. They suffer feelings of severe humiliation if forced to look at mistakes or imperfection.
7. Adults shamed as children frequently blame others before they can be blamed.
8. Adults shamed as children may suffer from debilitating guilt. These individuals apologize constantly. They assume responsibility for the behavior of those around them.
9. Adults shamed as children feel like outsiders. They feel a pervasive sense of loneliness throughout their lives, even when surrounded with those who love and care.
10. Adults shamed as children project their beliefs about themselves onto others. They engage in mind-reading . . . consistently feeling judged by others.
11. Adults shamed as children often feel angry and judgmental towards the qualities in others that they feel ashamed of in themselves. This can lead to shaming others.

12. Adults shamed as children often feel ugly, flawed and imperfect. These feelings regarding self may lead to focus on clothing and makeup in an attempt to hide flaws in personal appearance and self.
13. Adults shamed as children often feel controlled from the outside as well as from within. Normal spontaneous expression is blocked.
14. Adults shamed as children feel they must do things perfectly or not at all. This internalized belief frequently leads to performance anxiety and procrastination.
15. Adults shamed as children experience depression.
16. Adults shamed as children lie to themselves and others.
17. Adults shamed as children block their feelings of shame through compulsive behaviors like work-a-holism, eating disorders, shopping, and substance abuse, list-making or gambling.
18. Adults shamed as children often have caseloads rather than friendships.
19. Adults shamed as children often involve themselves in compulsive processing of past interactions and events and intellectualizations as a defense against pain.
20. Adult shamed as children are stuck in dependency or counter-dependency.
21. Adults shamed as children have little sense of emotional boundaries. They feel constantly violated by others. They frequently build false boundaries through walls, rage, pleasing or isolation.[1]

I can identify with almost all the above "Characteristics of Adults Shamed in Childhood." I continue, for example, to have problems with feedback from Helene even if it is positive and constructive. I immediately get defensive because I interpret it as shaming or criticizing me until I realize or Helene reminds me that she's not passing judgment on me but just offering some helpful information. This is how powerful an influence childhood shaming can carry over into adulthood.

I believe, without a doubt, that shaming is a form of emotional violence imposed on children. It is a destructive way that parents, teachers, preachers, siblings and others have of relating to us and controlling us (See Appendix B, "Never Good Enough . . .").

I'm grateful to a therapist who helped me overcome my shame. I have rid my life of all the "oughtas," "gottas," "have tos," and "shoulds" that others imposed on me and stunted my spiritual being. My therapist taught me to change my "I ought to," "got to," "have to" and "shoulds" to "I choose to," or "I choose not to." By making this change I am taking responsibility for my behavior rather than doing what others have imposed on me.

Jesus said the first of all the commandments is to "love the Lord your God with all your heart, and with all your soul, and with all your mind, and with all your strength." The second is this, you shall love your neighbor as yourself." (Mark 12: 30-31). By purging my shame I have learned to love myself and have become more spiritual.

Plays, poetry, music . . . the arts . . . are gifts of the spirit. Their messages lodge in our hearts and surface at times later in life when we need their instruction, insight, inspiration and healing.

Catherine Feste

~ 5 ~

RENEWING MOMENTS OF TRANSCENDENCE

We not only have a mystique or drive that leads us in search of meaning for our lives, we also have a spiritual hunger that craves renewed moments with the transcendent—those moments that surpass all human knowledge. Maslow said, ". . . man has a higher and transcendent nature, and this is part of his essence, i.e., his biological nature as a member of a species which has evolved."[1]

Abraham Maslow defined moments of transcendence as "peak" and "plateau experiences." Peak experiences as Maslow described them are "the best moments of human being . . . the happiest moments of life, . . . experiences of ecstasy, rapture, bliss, of greatest joy." [2]

Recovering addicts have the need for alternative highs to replace the addiction to the harmful highs they expected from their mood-altering drugs. I believe these alternative highs are similar to what Maslow defines as peak and plateau experiences.

Maslow differentiated between the plateau and peak experience. He believed the plateau experience always has an intellectual and cognitive element whereas the peak experience tends to be exclusively emotional.[3] Plateau experiences are ongoing rather than climactic. He distinguished further, saying:

> There is more an element of surprise, and of disbelief, and of esthetic shock in the peak experience, more the quality of having such an experience for the *first time* . . . Peak and plateau experiences differ also in their relations to death. The peak-experience can often meaningfully be called a "little death," and a rebirth in various senses. The less intense plateau-experience is more often experienced as pure enjoyment and happiness, as, let's say, in a mother sitting quietly looking, by the hour at her baby playing and marveling, wondering, philosophizing, not quite believing. She can experience this as a very pleasant, continuing, contemplative experience rather than as something akin to a climactic explosion which then ends.[4]

I've had peak-experiences through art, music, nature, meditation, and prayer. Let me illustrate some examples of nature's way of transcendence. I indicated in Chapter 2 that I was very close to my father-in-law, who became a father mentor to me. Bill was killed in a farming accident too early in his life. Several weeks after his funeral we were driving west, going home to visit my wife's mother. It was early evening when we came upon a beautiful sunset. I was overwhelmed with a feeling of peace and serenity and I sensed that all was well with my father-in-law—that he was in heaven.

For Henry David Thoreau, who fled civilization to live on Walden Pond, nature was the temple of God and the perennial source of life. A transcendent spiritual moment is the instant we are confronted with earth's perfection and are filled with awe. The scientist, Carl Sagan wrote about his time-in-nature experience: "The wind whips through the canyons of the American Southwest, and there is no one to hear it but us."

My son, Kevin, who is not religious but is deeply spiritual, loves the great outdoors. His Higher Power comes through nature. When he's hunting deer, he can sit in a tree stand for hours, alone. I stood in awe of him this last fall when he sat in his tree stand eleven hours for seven days before he got his first deer. He gets a natural high listening to the sounds and "music" of the forest and watching the animals go by his tree stand. I believe this is a transcendent experience for him.

I have undergone peak-experiences through prayer. There are so many things in life that I am totally powerless over. When I experience powerlessness I get stressed out and feel overwhelmed. How do I overcome these feelings of powerlessness? I say the Serenity: "God, grant me the serenity to accept the things I cannot change, the courage to change the things I can and the wisdom to know the difference." The end result is a feeling of inner peace and serenity.

Almost all world religions consider a form of prayer central to spirituality. "All the religions are true," said George Lucas, who played on religious themes such as good and evil in his blockbuster *Star War* series. "Religion is basically a container for faith. And faith is a very important part of what allows us to remain stable, remain balanced." I believe the mental and emotional release, along with a sense of connection to a higher power, may be at the heart of prayer's effectiveness.

Music and meditation are peak experiences for me. In fact, the above combination can relax and put me to sleep in just minutes. Music and meditation are also healthy. There is research documenting the effects of pleasant music on the brain. The studies revealed that it "deepens emotional experience, enhances visual and auditory processing and improves attention and the processing of emotions." [5]

"There is no greater source of strength and power for me in my life now than going still, being quiet and recognizing what real power is," said Oprah Winfrey on the segment of her daily show called, "Remembering Your Spirit." The Bible says, "Be still and know that I am God!" (Psalm 46: 9a). I experience that quietness and a power greater than myself in meditation and relaxation.

The above are just a few examples of transcendent, peak experiences. I've not only had peak experiences but I've had plateau experiences through dreams, exercise, gardening, hobbies and pets. Here are some examples that are more cognitive and intellectual versus a climactic, emotional experience.

Freud said, "dreams are the royal road to the unconscious." They are a means to completing the unfinished "business" in our lives that make us more whole. I had two dreams that helped me heal the pain of the abuse from my father. The first dream was not a plateau experience. In fact it was just the opposite. I found it to be very painful but essential to the transcendent dream.

I was in group therapy and our therapist asked us to bring a dream to the next session. I told him I didn't remember my dreams. He said that we often repress our painful memories and I needed to give myself permission to remember my dreams. That very next night I followed his instructions and had the following dream. I dreamed I was working in a gas station. When my father walked through the door I threw battery acid in his face and disfigured his face.

The next day I shared the dream in my group session. My Gestalt therapist informed me that every person, place, and thing in my dream was a part of my being. He told me to identify with the battery acid and share it in the first person here and now.

This is what I said: "I am battery acid and . . . . my father is walking through the door . . . I am taking the battery acid and I'm throwing it in his face . . . and . . . disfiguring his face." I found this experience so painful that it took considerable time and help from my therapist for me to work through the places I was blocking. Before I finished I got in touch with all the hurt from my father's abuse. I cried uncontrollably for what seemed like an eternity.

My therapist suggested I write a letter to my father in which I listed all of my past resentments of him. When I finished listing those I was instructed to convert all of my resentments into appreciations—a difficult task I can assure you! When I had completed my letter of resentments and appreciations I was to forgive my father for not being a perfect parent. I went home and shared my letter with my father. I was pleased because that was the beginning of reconciliation. (See Appendix C, "A Letter to My Father").

Although the above dream and letter helped me express the pain from my past. I wasn't finished yet. Several weeks later I had a related dream that was, what I believe, a plateau experience. This dream not only helped me finish the unfinished issues in my life but was a healing power that made me more whole spiritually.

I dreamed I was on a battle field shooting at the enemy. My father was covering my back side and was shooting at the enemy when he was shot. This is where my dream seemed to get weird. After he was shot, he fell into a fiery volcano. Shortly thereafter, what appeared to be communion wafers—came exploding out of the volcano and one fell in my mouth. I consumed it and felt totally at peace with my father.

I interpreted this dream on my own. I said, "I'm on a battle field and I'm shooting at the enemy. My father is covering my back side. He is shot, falls into a volcano and is exploding out of the volcano in communion wafers. One wafer is falling in my mouth. I am consuming it and I am feeling at peace with my father."

I have reflected on this experience several times since and I continue to experience inner peace and serenity. Without a doubt, I had a plateau experience.

I've had plateau-experiences from woodworking and gardening. Furniture, toys, bird and butterfly houses are just a few of the things I create. Creating something I can visualize and admire is both a cognitive and emotional experience for me. This is true for gardening as well. Growing a beautiful garden can be a transcendent experience. It renews my heart, mind, and soul. Our daughter, Kathy, who is a seasoned and prolific gardener will testify to the above. John Denver, in his "Garden Song," spoke to the spiritual aspect of gardening. (See "Appendix D, "Garden Song" by John Denver).

I've included pets as a plateau-experience which may seem a bit strange for those of you who are not pet owners. My French Poodle has all the qualities of a caring, Higher Power. In fact, dog is God spelled backward. Animals have many spiritual qualities and teach us a lot about spirituality. (See Appendix E, "Animals as Spiritual Guides").

Our greatest need is not to find happiness but meaning for our lives. I believe experiencing moments of transcendence, whether peak or plateau experiences, can bring us both happiness and meaning. In addition, the memories of those "mountain" peak experiences will carry us through the "valleys" in life.

Values are actually a very special power in the universe. It is one our minds can grasp for the purpose of *uplifting* life. Values are actually *spiritual skills*—a divine gift that comes from the infinite source of things.

Roy Posner—The Power of Personal Values

~ 6 ~

HAVING CONGRUENT VALUES

What happened to our values? Increasingly, we are living in a world that doesn't seem to value acts of conscience. False doctrines of greed, hatred and materialism have permeated our world to such an extent that standing for what is right often looks and sounds outdated. And yet, values are essential to spiritual and physical wholeness.

Maslow wrote, "The human needs a framework of values, a philosophy of life . . . to live by and understand by, in about the same sense that he needs sunlight, calcium, or love."[1]

Values, according to Dr. Clinebell "are biological necessities for avoiding illness and achieving one's full potential."[2] He concluded:

> The epidemic of spiritual illnesses . . . resulting from deprivation of these values include anomie, alienation, meaninglessness, loss of zest for life, hopelessness, boredom, and axiological depression . . . Chronic problems in living always reflect distorted or impoverished values in need of revision." [3]

Values guide how I live, what has meaning to me—what I stand for. When I violate my values, I violate myself and others. Let me illustrate from my personal life. I will never forget the night I discovered that our seventeen-year-old son was a drug addict. But the real shock was learning that our fifteen-year-old daughter was also hooked on drugs.

We were in a chemically dependent treatment center with our son, Kevin, when we became suspicious of our daughter, Kathy. She had been depressed for some time and had been isolating in her bedroom. She refused to share any information about Kevin's drug use which indicated she was trying to protect and cover up her own drug use.

Our counselor suggested we contract with Kathy to stay sober for two weeks and if she broke the contract, she should come in for an evaluation. She agreed to the contract and the second night of her contract she got "high."

She had been extremely depressed that evening and was isolating in her room. She finally came out of isolation, said she was going for a walk and would be back shortly. She came back about one hour later, giggling and acting like nothing was wrong.

When she came home she refused to look me in the eye, went directly to her room and shut the door. I followed her to her room, asked her if she was "high" and she confessed she was. The following morning I took her in for an evaluation and she was admitted to the drug unit for further evaluation.

I was furious! I felt overwhelmed with resentment and self-pity. Why me, I asked? Why do I have two children who are drug addicts? I felt like a wounded bird. My body, mind and spirit seemed shattered.

My emotions were out of control. Like a yo-yo, they were bouncing from one extreme to another. One moment I was screaming in rage and the next I was sobbing. I felt fragile and delicate—like a dandelion in the seed stage where only a tiny puff of wind would have the power to strew and scatter my whole life into many parts. I really thought I was going crazy and needed to be admitted to a mental health unit.

In the midst of my brokenness and pain, someone said to me: "Ken, have you considered doing a fearless and searching, moral inventory?"—the Fourth Step of Alcoholics Anonymous. I took that person's advice and probably saved myself a lot of medical bills.

But greater yet, that was the beginning of my spiritual recovery.

As I was writing my moral inventory I became aware of how much I had violated my values. I was feeling overwhelmed with guilt, shame and resentments. These powerful feelings were reminders that my behavior was not congruent with my values.

There is a civil war of values that happens, not only in the alcoholic or drug addict but also with the family members that live with the alcoholic.

I felt like the Apostle Paul when he said, "I do not understand my own actions. For I do not do what I want, but I do the very thing I hate."

I wrote example after example of things I should not have done. Honesty is one of my highest values and I remembered the many times I lied to cover up my son's using behavior.

One night, when Kevin was using drugs, he came home drunk and skipped school the next day. He asked me to write a note for his school stating the reason he missed school was because he was sick. And I did! I should have written, "My son was absent because he was nursing a hang-over. Please give him whatever consequence you think is appropriate."

I am a non-violent person and I have a high respect and value for life. However, I will never forget the night I violated my value of compassion. I was getting ready for bed when I discovered Kevin had left the garage door open. I politely asked him to close it but he refused. We got into a fierce argument and he called me some names I wouldn't want to print. I exploded in a fit of rage, grabbed him by the throat and started choking him. I was on the verge of killing my son. My guilt was overwhelming.

Abuse, both verbal and physical, happens frequently in chemically-dependent families. But I was a loving father who lost control because of the "cunning, baffling and powerful"[4] nature of the illness.

Families have the need for fun. Laughter and play are essential to a healthy spirituality. Someone said, "The best gift we can give our children is happy memories." Our family didn't have many happy memories during our illness. Instead of having fun we were arguing and fighting.

The name-calling, the things I did in rage, the threats and the lying were extreme violations of my value system. I was guilty and needed to "admit to God, myself and another human being the exact nature of my wrongs." Through the process of admitting my wrongs to a priest, my Higher Power (God), and myself, I not only saw how I had violated my values but also felt forgiven and accepted just as I am.

I am becoming more spiritually mature because the pain of my guilt has enabled me to become congruent with my values again. Guilt is a healthy warning signal that tells me I have violated my values. When I heed the warning signal I can admit I am wrong, change my behavior and conform to my values. This is one spiritual pathway that bring inner peace and spiritual wholeness.

Trust has to be earned, and should come only after the passage of time.

Arthur Ashe

~7~
TRUSTING AND BEING TRUSTED

Don't trust, don't talk, don't feel was characteristic of our family when our children became alcoholics and drug addicts. We never wanted to talk about what had happened. It was like having an elephant in the middle of the living room and everyone tip-toed around it as though it were not there. We didn't trust the world with our secret let alone trust each other.

Don't trust, don't talk, don't feel was the law our family lived by, and God help the one who broke it. I remember how angry my uncle felt when he read my book, *Addicted to the Addict*. I had exposed our family secret that my paternal grandfather was an alcoholic. As he saw it, I had betrayed a sacred trust and how dare I lie about his father. He was in a state of denial!

On the other hand, there is a genuine trust that is violated when a family suffers from the disease of chemical dependency. Words cannot describe the fear I felt the day we brought our son, Kevin, home from in-patient, chemical dependency treatment. As we waited nervously for the elevator to take us to the lobby, my stomach felt like it was tied in knots. My mind was racing with thoughts of, "What if Kevin starts using drugs again?", "Can I really trust him not to use again?"

Our family therapist informed us that Kevin would have to earn our trust back and it would probably be some time before we could fully trust him again. We had been wounded deeply by his drug-related behavior. Vernon Johnson, an Episcopal priest and recovered alcoholic devoted his life to alcohol intervention, wrote, "The cost of trusting another whose behavior has a history of being untrustworthy is to take the risk of being hurt . . . . again."[1]

The lying, manipulating, cheating, stealing, abusive behavior of the drug addict is not quickly forgotten and taking the risk of getting hurt one more time was not going to be easy either. Could I, for example, trust my son to drive a car again? He had three car accidents within two weeks when he was using—one was a hit-and-run accident. Could my wife and I go on a vacation and trust that our son would not invite his using friends to our home for a party and trash our house?

Our week of family therapy seemed to have only opened the wounds I had suffered from my son's betrayal. My vivid, painful memories haunted me for a long time after treatment. My trust had been violated and I wrestled whether I wanted to forgive my son. Forgiving him meant I might get hurt one more time. Mechtild of Magdeburg, a Roman Catholic sister and a medieval mystic, wrote:

> From suffering I have learned this: That whoever is sore wounded by love will never be made whole unless she embraces the very same love which wounded her. [2]

She was right! For me not to forgive meant I would live with my anger and resentment. If I hang onto resentments it only makes me a slave to that person forever. I give away all my power to the person I resent and that person is in control of me.

We don't wait for the person who wounded us to apologize. The other person may never offer that apology and be reconciled with us. Forgiveness is for the benefit of the person who is wounded. In order for me to be made whole again I needed to "embrace the very same love that wounded me"—i.e. forgive my son for not being a perfect son.

When I refuse to forgive I wound my spirituality. I assume a self-righteous attitude that I am without fault or incapable of wrongdoing. In fact, I assume a god-like position and in doing so I deny my own weaknesses and faults. If I scapegoat others by focusing on their faults I can avoid looking at my own weaknesses and thereby, stunt my own personal growth.

Janis Spring, a Diplomat in Clinical Psychology and author of <u>How Can I Forgive You</u>, wrote:

> Not forgiving may restore your pride, but it cuts you off from an opportunity for personal growth and understanding. When you refuse to forgive, you transfer all the blame to the offender and make yourself unassailable. This proud pretense of perfection, however, is likely to mask a shaky interior.... Wrapped in sanctimonious anger, never questioning how you may be wrong, you cut yourself off from an opportunity to look into yourself—to learn, change, and grow.[3]

My self-righteous attitude was shattered one night in family therapy. The family therapist confronted me with, "Mr. Reiners, you need to stop taking your son's inventory and start looking at your own behavior."

I was reminded of Jesus' words to the self-righteous, religious leaders of his day:

> Do not judge, so that you may not be judged. Why do you see the speck in your neighbor's eye, but do not notice the log that is in your own eye? ... You hypocrite, first take the log out of your own eye, and then you will see clearly to take the speck out of your neighbor's eye. (Matthew 7: 1-5).

My son had violated our relationship but I too, was guilty of wounding him by my behavior. I had said things out of rage I wish I hadn't said. I had screamed abusive, discounting words that had hurt him deeply

I was guilty of violating my values and I needed to earn my trust with Kevin just as he had to earn his trust with me. Trust is a two-way street, according to Dr. Freeman, Doctor of Clinical Psychology, "The only way to make a man trustworthy is to trust him."[4]

Kevin and I had to learn how to trust each other again by changing our behavior. We had violated the values that we learned for trusting and being trusted. Therefore, we had to become congruent with our values again. We now have a loving, positive relationship and enjoy each other's company. In the following chapter we will discover how trust and being trusted is vital to joining caring and nurturing communities.

One of the marvelous things about community is that it enables us to welcome and help people in a way we couldn't do as individuals. When we pool our strengths and share the work and responsibility, we can welcome many people, even those in deep distress and perhaps help them find self-confidence and inner healing.

Jean Vanier—<u>Community and Growth</u>

~ 8 ~
JOINING CARING AND NURTURING COMMUNITIES

Spiritual wholeness cannot be achieved without belonging to a caring and nurturing community. Dr. Clinebell wrote:

> Spiritual growth occurs most rapidly in a group committed to spiritual values. This can only take place in a two-person group, like a deep friendship or creative marriage. It can be in a small spiritual growth group of persons committed to nurturing ethical and spiritual discovery. It can be in a church or a temple where there is both that warm caring and refreshing openness that allows the growth formula to come alive in relationships . . . . It is in communities of mutual caring that the fullest possible liberation of spiritual potentials takes place. [1]

Trust is vital to spiritual growth in a caring and nurturing community. If I cannot trust or be trusted, spiritual growth will not happen. There's always the possibility that someone can violate our trust but if we want to grow spiritually, we need to take the risk of getting hurt. The alternative is loneliness, isolation and detachment which ultimately leads to death. "Basic human needs," according to Dr. Maslow, "can be fulfilled *only* by and through other human beings." [2]

Health and healing happens in caring and nurturing communities. An individual does not become whole in isolation, but only in relationship to others. We need the love and care of others to overcome our hurt and pain whether it be psychological or physical. I personally have experienced both psychological and physical healing through caring and nurturing communities. I have given several examples throughout this book.

My low self-esteem began to heal as I experienced unconditional love from my father-in-law. As Scott Peck wrote, "for our mental and spiritual growth we must develop our own personal religion and not rely on that of our parents."[3]

Being congruent with my values is a biological necessity for avoiding illness. Confessing my character defects to God, myself and a priest helped me discover how my codependency had contributed to the illness of my son and daughter. In addition it helped me become aware of my true values again.

I took seven quarters of Clinical Pastoral Education where I was in a group of my peers and I got feedback from them regarding personal and pastoral identity. Through the group process I was able to clarify and gain a clearer identity in my personal life and pastoral role.

Parent's Al-Anon helped me let go of my controlling nature and freed me to become a more loving, responsible parent. The group helped me let go of my inappropriate guilt I had in thinking my mistakes as a father had caused my son and daughter's illness.

All the above spiritual and mental healing happened through the process of caring and nurturing communities. Furthermore, I have also experienced physical healing from caring and nurturing groups. There's an African adage that states, "Where there's a thorn in the foot, the whole body stoops to pull it out."

The above adage was true when I suffered a severe, head injury on March 7, 1999. My wife, Helene, and I flew to Greece and boarded a ship to begin our tour of Turkey. The first seven days of our tour we visited the ruins of the cities where the Apostle Paul had established the first Christian churches in Europe. On the seventh day of our journey we left the ship to go on a land tour of Athens. We had to walk the ship's gang-plank and step down into a boat tender which took us to shore. As I stepped into the boat tender I bumped my head on a low, overhead, iron crossbar.

Three days later I had a headache and begun losing control of my balance when I was walking down Mars Hill after seeing the world-renowned Acropolis and the Parthenon. That evening I went into a coma. Three Minnesota physicians in our tour examined me at our hotel and recommended that Helene have me hospitalized immediately. I was diagnosed as having an acute, subdural hematoma and had a craniotomy surgery at Athen's hospital.

While Helene was waiting a Greek man came into the waiting room. He had brought his sister in because of heart problems. It so happened that he was the only English speaking Greek person in the waiting room. He introduced himself to Helene and told her to call him "George" because his name was too difficult for her to pronounce. He told Helene that he would interpret what the Greek doctors were telling her about my condition.

Helene told him she had to call our children in the states to tell them of my accident and that I might die but she didn't know how to do that since she couldn't speak or understand Greek. George handed her his cell phone and dialed our daughter's number.

He overheard Helene tell our daughter that she had only $300.00 of Greek drachma which was worth about thirty cents in American money. We had spent most of our Greek money because we were scheduled to leave for home the morning I had surgery. George gave Helene enough Greek money to tide her over until our daughter arrived. When she wanted to pay him back, he refused and said, "We Greeks are not that way."

The above takes on even greater significance because of the fact that the U.S. was bombing Kosovo while we were there and the Greek people were angry at our country because of the bombing. They were rioting at the U.S. Embassy just two blocks from the hotel where Helene was staying. Yet, here was a generous and compassionate, Greek man in spite of our military action in Kosovo.

Our group tour, made up of clergy and members of the United Methodist churches throughout the state of Minnesota, had ended the night before I was admitted to the hospital. We were told later that they prayed for my recovery as they were flying home the next morning. Also the various churches of the members on the tour continued to pray for me. Helene had a network of business clients throughout the United States that prayed for my recovery as well.

I am convinced, without a doubt, that I would not be alive today had it not been for all the communities that assisted me in my recovery. Furthermore, I also believe, without a doubt, prayer helped in my healing and recovery. Research has revealed when prayer is practiced within the context of weekly religious activity, many health benefits have been found including living longer.[4]

Dr. Ira Tanner, author of The Fear of Love, wrote, "Who needs people? It's like a tree saying, who needs the soil? or a fish, 'Who needs water?"[5] A caring and nurturing community is essential to survival as a tree needs soil or a fish needs water. That is why I'm alive today, both spiritually and physically.

Spiritual wholeness does not always come easy or without pain. Dr. Kennedy, Roman Catholic priest and psychologist wrote, "Wisdom seems to come to men more from disappointment and hurt than from knowledge and kindness."[6] Alcoholics Anonymous has a saying, "No pain, No gain." Someone has written:

> The rift in the chest of a mountain
> The twist in the trunk of the tree,
> The water cut cave in the hollow,
> The rough, rocky rim of the sea . . .
> Each one has a scar of distortion
> Yet each has this sermon to sing
> "The presence of what would deface me,
> Has made me a beautiful thing.

My spiritual journey has not been without suffering but confronting the pain has enabled me to become more spiritually whole.

The Higher Self is that part of you that connects you directly to the spiritual realms. It is eternal, infinitely wise and transcends your everyday consciousness. It is in touch with the Divine because it is part of it. Attaining knowledge of the Higher Self, and its depths of inner wisdom, is the goal of the Spiritual Quest . . .

Asoka Selvarajah—<u>Who is the Higher Self?</u>

∴ 9 ∴

DEVELOPING OUR HIGHER SELF

A healthy spirituality requires that we develop our higher self. Dr. Clinebell equates higher self with what traditional religious language called the soul. He defines and explains higher self by speaking from his own experience. He wrote:

> As a client in a session with a therapist trained in psychosynthesis, I had been struggling futilely to resolve some hard lumps of grief and anger within me. For a variety of reasons, I was getting nowhere in my attempts to liberate myself from these. The turning point came when the therapist invited me to get in touch with my higher self—'the place within you where you are whole and together'—and to see the issues with which I had been struggling from that perspective. When I did this, the cold lumps seemed to melt. My depression and sense of entrapment lifted as I felt a flow of energy within. [1]

I believe that in most instances we get in touch with our higher self and grow spiritually when we can gain wisdom from and heal the brokenness in our lives. Eugene Kennedy, professor of psychology at Loyola University in Chicago, wrote:

> It is strange that what is truly beautiful about man is revealed only if we are strong enough to look at his scars. There is, in fact, no way to understand strength without understanding weakness, no way to live life whole unless we face up to its hard truths. [2]

I have developed and continue to develop my higher self by facing up to the hard truths I have encountered in my life. I have revealed in the previous chapters how I've grown spiritually from the scars I suffered in my life.

In Chapter 2 I revealed how I developed my higher, intellectual self by casting out the monster God instilled in me by my parent's religious teachings. I came to believe in a loving, higher power by experiencing unconditional love through my father-in-law and from what I learned in college and divinity school.

In Chapter 3 I shared how I developed my higher self by learning to live a more positive philosophy of life. My continuing education has freed me from the negative conditioning I learned from my father and the negative brainwashing I learned from religion.

I have not fully escaped my negative thinking and occasionally slip into it but I can catch myself now and turn a negative into a positive. No one develops their higher self fully in their life time. In fact, it is a life time process and varies according to how deeply one is wounded and if they can heal their wounds.

In Chapter 4 I revealed how shame imposed on me by others was destructive to my higher self. I suffered from low self-esteem and thought I was a bad person and worthless.

I spent many hours in therapy ridding myself of shame that bound me to negativity and loneliness because I feared intimacy. I am grateful to my therapist for helping me free myself from the shame that bound me. It enabled me to develop my higher self further.

Our need for ongoing peak experiences (Chapter 5) is essential for happiness. Dream therapy was a transcendent experience for me and enabled me to rid myself of the repressed rage I carried towards my father for years because of his abuse. Rage and anger are secondary feelings which block out the primary, positive feelings. Letting go of the rage helped me get in touch with the more genuine, positive feelings such as joy, love, awe, caring, serenity, worthiness.

When I was in dream therapy my therapist gave me an assignment. He asked me to go home, take my father to lunch and, sometime during the course of our conversation, ask him, "What do you remember most about my growing up as a child?" He responded, without hesitation, "I remember that no matter how hard I punished you, you never cried." I had learned to shut off all my feelings, except rage, when I was a child.

I developed my higher, emotional self when I learned to feel my genuine feelings. I cannot express in words how much I feel alive as the result of being able to express my true feelings. Furthermore, I have been able to experience more transcendent moments because I can feel again.

Living within the framework of my values (Chapter 6), has enabled me to work on developing my full potential. Values are essential guidelines for guilt-free living. If I violate my values I will feel guilty reminding me I need to get back on track again. Relieved of the burden of guilt gives me energy to enjoy life more fully and develop my higher self.

In Chapter 7, I share from my personal experience how trust is essential in building wholesome relationships. Trust must be earned by being honest and open in our relationships. But trust also has to be given away with no conditions. To not trust leads to loneliness and isolation which is destructive to my higher self and leads to spiritual death.

John Donne, English clergyman and poet said "No man is an island, entire of itself . . . any man's death diminishes me, because I am involved in mankind; and therefore never send to know for whom the bell tolls; it tolls for thee." We need others to develop our higher self (Chapter 8). Community fulfills our basic human needs. We need the love, openness and honesty of others to facilitate mental and physical healing. I have been involved in many different communities that have enabled me to grow spiritually—Al-Anon, Dream therapy group, Clinical Pastoral Education group, Men's Therapy group, Grief group—to name a few.

I said in the introduction of my book that "As I grow older I find myself growing less religious and more spiritual." I hope sharing my spiritual journey will help you grow more spiritual. Frederick Buechner, an American writer and a ordained Presbyterian minister, concludes that in someone's story we may catch a glimpse of ourselves. He wrote:

> My assumption is that the story of any one of us is in some measure the story of us all . . . . even in a stranger's album, there is always the possibility that as the pages flip by, on one of them you may even catch a glimpse of yourself . . . . a third possibility . . . . is that once I have put away my album for good, you may in the privacy of the heart take out the album of your own life and search it for the people and places you have loved and learned from yourself, and for those moments in the past . . . . through which you glimpsed . . . . the sacredness of your own journey.[3]

Blessings on your sacred, spiritual journey.

APPENDIX A

A Letter From an Atheist

Ch. K. Reiners
St. Mary's Rehabilitation Center
2512 South Seventh Street
Minneapolis, Minn. 55454

Dear Ken—

I wanted to express my appreciation for your counseling during our just completed Family Week. To say that that week changed my life and my husband's and my joint outlook on life would be an understatement.

It was at your lecture on Friday morning when the events of the entire week—during which you knew I suffered greatly—came together. I found your philosophies and explanations profoundly helpful and your lecture one which I thought anyone—devout Catholic, Orthodox Jew, confirmed Protestant, agnostic or atheist—could relate to! I was appreciative of your sharing of your personal experiences—suddenly we were not uniquely suffering parents wondering how two such incompatible people could ever have come together. We entered the week as two separate, unfriendly argumentative individuals. We passed through such misery during the week that the possibility of continuing 28 ½ year marriage became almost non-existent. We ended the week as two loving, caring, supportive people, united in outlook and a desire to perpetuate this new-found warmth.

Despite the fact that the problems have not changed, weight has been lifted from our shoulders by the knowledge we gained at St. Mary's this week and our newly regained mutual support for each other. You are doing valuable work—you know that, but you may not be aware of how effective you have been. I wanted you to know that I am appreciative.

Sincerely, Jen Z

*The lecture indicated in the above letter was a lecture on Higher Power.

To Kwiecien, who admits that shaming and emotional abuse are elusive concepts, the final test remains concrete: "If you can't raise your child to be a responsible adult with a good self-image," she says, "then that's emotional abuse. It's the bruises that don't show that often take the longest to heal. Without help, the victims of shaming's bruises never do."

Author Unknown

APPENDIX B

NEVER GOOD ENOUGH: THE LEGACY OF SHAME

There is a kind of family violence that doesn't leave scars and isn't a secret. It happens in grocery stores, in the neighbor's yard, in the cousin's house. Witnessing it may bring about in the onlooker a vague sense of discomfort, but none of the revulsion and outrage that physical or sexual abuse inspires. Yet this kind of family violence may cause more human misery and cripple more lives than any other form.

The violence is shaming, a form of emotional violence we inflict on our children, sometimes without even realizing it. But we must learn to recognize it because its consequences are grave and its victims are everywhere.

"The experience of shame is the piercing awareness of ourselves as fundamentally deficient in some vital way as a human being," writes Gershen Kaufman, the Michigan State University professor who first defined the problem in his book, "Shame, the Power of Caring." "To live with shame is to experience the very essence or heart of the self as wanting."

Shaming is a destructive way that parents have of relating to their children and controlling them. It begins "even before the kids are walking," says Hennepin County domestic court family counselor, Karen Shaud. Even before he can talk, a child can develop shame if a parent refuses to respond to the child's need for physical holding and comfort.

Kaufman stresses that when emotional hurts cause a child to seek physical comforting, words of "reassurance may not be sufficient to reaffirm the child's inner well-being."

To have our physical and emotional needs met helps us to develop trust and transmits to us a sense of self-worth, says University of Minnesota family, social science instructor, Susan Kwiecien. When this does not happen, the result is often shame. "Shame filled people feel that something is wrong at their very core . . . . It is a sense of being bad that pervades lives," says Kwiecien.

An extreme example of the consequences of denying this very human need for loving touch was seen in the 19th century orphanages where children failed to thrive, though their physical needs were met. In most babies, the physical manifestations of the denial of holding are not this extreme, but shaming may have already begun its insidious course.

As a child begins to talk at about age two, her next important step is to develop a positive sense of identity. That is essentially the opposite of a shame-filled identity, and the parental styles responsible for both are quite different.

The sources of shaming or the ways in which parents go about causing their children to become shame-filled are many. The most blatant forms of inducing shame are the most obvious—physical and sexual abuse. "Being physically attacked or sexually abused is a shaming experience by its very definition," says Shaud.

But constant yelling and criticism are as emotionally destructive and probably more widespread because they are more accepted by society in general. "Sometimes I feel pretty pessimistic about shaming," says Shaud. "I go to Target and I see kids having really terrible days because their parents are so shaming and punitive. Constant yelling and criticism is a violation of a child's personhood."

Performance expectations by adults of their children are also a common source of shame, Kaufman says. Unreasonable expectations come from a parent who is herself so shame-filled that anything the child does is seen as reflecting on her rather than on the child.

Performance expectations illustrate an element of shaming that is common to all forms of family violence—that is a cycle, a legacy, passed on from parent to child. It is common for "strategies of transfer" to take place within shame-filled people, Kaufman says. These strategies" aim at making someone else feel shame in order to reduce their own shame," he writes.

Transfer strategies can take the form of rage, contempt, striving for power, striving for perfection, transferring blame, and internal withdrawal. They are all unconsciously used by shame-filled adults to pass their shame on, usually to their children. "Shame is a family phenomenon, not an individual one, says family therapist, Marilyn Mason of St. Paul's Family Therapy Institute in St. Paul, Minnesota. "Shame," she says "begets shame."

One common family manifestation of shame, says Mason, is the over-involved, totally enmeshed family, in which the parents are over-protective and give the children no freedom to learn, hence developing in them a sense of inadequacy. Another is the chaotic or separate family, in which the parents give their children no boundaries at all, making them feel unimportant.

"Being a healthy parent," says Shaud, "means being firm but nurturing, giving children a decent sense of boundaries along with lots of unconditional love." Unconditional love—the feeling that one is loved for oneself and not for what one does or doesn't do—is an important part of a healthy growth, says Kwiecien.

Shame-filled kids are raised by parents who attribute the wrong or bad things they do to that kid as a bad person rather than separating out the behavior from the person," she says. For example, if a child throws a tantrum, it's important for the parents to say, "What you did was wrong but I know you are basically a good person," Kwiecien emphasizes. She adds. "Kids don't want to be bad. They have a great need to be responded to positively."

Sometimes shame, in a family, is centered in what counselors call family secrets. Out-of-wedlock pregnancies, unresolved grief, mental illness, and financial failure are among the most common family secrets, says Mason. "Shame is transferred through secrets and darkness," she says. "Family members feel something is wrong with them but they don't know quite what."

If those secrets can be brought into the light and discussed, their power is reduced. "As a counselor, I find that if you don't pass that secret, that shame, back to your parents, you will pass it on to your kids."

But much shame isn't based on a family secret but rather on the way that parents bring up their children so that those children don't feel good about themselves. "Those who don't get help will feel much despair," says Shaud. "They will always feel defective as a person, different somehow, from everyone else."

In her work, Shaud has identified three processes that help reduce shame. The first, of course, is family therapy, which she feels must be long-term therapy of about two to three years in duration with a therapist who looks at the origin of the shame and helps the patient to rebuild a positive identity.

Spiritual pursuits, such as involvement in organized religion, also seem to help many people, Shaud says. "At its best, religion gives people hope," she says. "The message of Christianity . . . is that you are cherished and loved as a person no matter what." This message is of great comfort to shame-filled people who have never heard it from their parents, Shaud explains.

Finally, organizations like Alcoholics Anonymous, with its 12 Steps to a new life, are helpful, says Shaud. They move people from a shame-based identity (I am bad and there's nothing to be done about it), to a guilt-based identity (I have bad behavior but can change it if I want to).

All three counselors emphasize that talking about the shame helps to purge it and reduces its power. This isn't easy, however. "It's very difficult to get shame-filled people into therapy," says Kwiecien, "because they can't be vulnerable and it just increases their shame to admit that they need help."

But dealing with shame is crucial. "The more I think about it, the more I think that almost all emotional and psychological difficulties are related to shame," says Shaud, who in her work as a court counselor, sees many families twisted and breaking under shame's strain. Shame's "rigid defending strategies," says Kaufman," produce distorted relationships with others, creating new pressures."

The irony is that a shame-filled person, whose greatest need is to feel loved for himself, keeps away and destroys the very thing that he needs most—an intimate relationship. "Shame filled people can't be vulnerable or real," says Kwiecien. "They want you to buy their facade. You can't have an intimate relationship with a shame-based person."

Shame then, is a terrible legacy to give a child. It is an insidious destroyer of what is best in life—accepting oneself and loving others.

Therapists feel strongly that shaming can be every bit as devastating as the more publicized forms of physical and sexual child abuse.

APPENDIX C

A LETTER TO MY FATHER

April 26, 1973
Dear Dad:

    Yesterday I shared one of my dreams in a Gestalt seminar group and Wow!! What an experience it was!! I became aware of the intensity of an unfinished situation with you. It emerged like Mt. Vesuvius as I cried uncontrollably. I realized that I have never really let you in on my feelings about you. Worse yet, for thirty years I have stockpiled my resentments towards you. God! How unfair I've been with you!

    I can't imprison those feelings any longer. They are screaming for release—to be driven out. And I want to share those resentments with you <u>now</u> dad. I want to share those feelings so I can forgive you and stop blaming you for not being a <u>perfect</u> parent. I am letting go of you so I can no longer use you as an excuse for the way I am. Here they are:

    I <u>resent</u> you for all the times you put me down with your anger. I <u>resent</u> you for not holding me on your lap and embracing me and kissing me. I <u>resent</u> you for not playing with me and spending some time alone with me. I <u>resent</u> you for forcing me to go to church and to listen to those daily devotions when I didn't understand them I <u>resent</u> you for not allowing me to play football in high school. I <u>resent</u> you for the way you put down others with your critical remarks. I <u>resent</u> you for not listening to me. I demand you hear me now!

And now that I have shared my resentments with you, I want you to know that <u>I forgive you</u> for not being the perfect parent and not living up to my expectations for you. And, furthermore, I want you to know that I <u>appreciate</u> your ability to express your anger openly to me because it set limits for me, and I always knew your limits. I <u>appreciate</u> your not holding me on your lap and embracing and kissing me because it has made me more aware of how much I need to do this to my son, my daughter, and my wife.

I <u>appreciate</u> your not playing with me because it has made me aware of how important it is for me to spend more time with Kevin and Kathy. I <u>appreciate</u> your forcing me to go to church and to listen to the daily devotions after dinner because it has brought me into a deeper and more significant understanding of what religion is all about—it has brought a deeper meaning to my life. Better yet, it has given me life for a second time.

I <u>appreciate</u> you for not allowing me to play football in high-school because it allowed me more time to play at home. I <u>appreciate</u> you for being critical because it has enabled me to be more sensitive to other person's feelings and to not always accept things as they are. I <u>appreciate</u> your not listening to me at times for it has encouraged me to try and be a better listener. And, I believe what I <u>appreciate</u> most about you is your sense of humor and your earthiness because it has enabled me to be less serious and to enjoy life more. I <u>appreciate</u> you for giving me life the first time.

And I believe I am now experiencing the re-birth of a second life. I no longer feel the need to be dependent on you. The following quotation has become my prayer and sums up the way I feel right now:

> "I do my thing and you do your thing. I am not in this world to live up to your expectation and you are not in this world to live up to mine. You are you and I am I, and if, by chance, we find each other, it's beautiful. If not, it can't be helped."

P. S. I can't remember the last time I shared this with you, but I want to share it now:

"I LOVE YOU!"

Your son,

Ken

APPENDIX D
GARDEN SONG—JOHN DENVER

Inch by inch, row by row
Gonna make this garden grow
All it takes is a rake and a hoe
And a piece of fertile ground.

Inch by inch, row by row
Someone bless these seeds I sow
Someone warm them from below
Till the rain comes tumblin' down.

Pullin' weeds and pickin' stones
Man is made of dreams and bones
Feel the need to grow my own
'Cause the time is close at hand.

Rainful rain, sun and rain
Find my way in nature's chain
Tune my body and my brain
To the music from the land.

Plant your rows straight and long
Temper them with prayer and song

Ken Reiners

> Mother Earth will make you strong
> If you give her love and care.
>
> Old crow watchin' hungrily
> From his perch in yonder tree
> In my garden I'm as free
> As that feathered thief up there.

Words and music by Dave Mallett

APPENDIX E

ANIMALS AS SPIRITUAL GUIDES BY KEN REINERS

Animals are a lot smarter than we give them credit for and they can teach us much about spirituality. Animals teach us that it is good to be an animal. They do not hesitate to demonstrate their joy in living. Some of the happiest creatures are animals. For example, my dog greets me when I come home by jumping up and down with great enthusiasm. He also takes great pride in his new haircut.

Animals teach us how to be a true friend. My dog is always there for me when I need him. My dog knows when I feel sad and will jump on my lap and kiss my face. Someone said, "One reason a dog can be such a comfort when you're feeling blue is that he doesn't try to find out why." They don't judge you or question you. My dog can also feel my happiness and get just as goofy as I can when I'm happy.

Animals teach us humility. When two wolves are in a fight, for example, and one is about to be killed, the defeated wolf will lift his head and bare his throat to his opponent. The opponent becomes incapacitated and he cannot kill the other wolf as long as he's faced with this tactic.

Animals teach us that play is an adult thing to do and needs no justification. My dog loves to play ball. I can toss a ball to him and he catches it in his mouth. He will chase his tail just for the fun of it.

Animals teach us to trust in a higher power. They are always true and faithful to their master. When they are lost they can find their way home again. They will defend you and protect you from harm. They accept you just as you are. If I get cross or scold my dog he still loves me.

Animals teach us that solitude is okay. I have been amazed to learn how many animals come out to watch the sunset. Who cannot be impressed and awed by the eagle that soars solo in the sky.

Animals can heal us. Alan Beck and Aaron Katcher have documented the therapeutic benefits of animal companionship:

> Patients who are unwilling to approach or talk to a therapist are able to reach out to an animal. After playing with, touching, and talking to the animal they begin to talk to humans again.[1]

Beck and Katcher reported other findings:

1. Almost everybody with a pet talks to it as if it were a person and the way people talk to cats, dogs, and birds resembles the way we talk to infants.
2. While talking to people usually raises blood pressure, sometimes to very high levels the touch-talk dialogue we establish with pets reduces stress and lowers blood pressure.
3. Just having a pet in a room makes people feel safer and lowers blood pressure.
4. People with pets make fewer doctor visits.
5. Pets can coax smiles and words out of socially withdrawn institutionalized patients of all ages.
6. Pets can make psychotherapy progress faster.[2] Further, relationships with animals have also been shown to have favorable effects on patients with heart disease. Studies conducted from 1977 to 1979 at the University of Maryland found that pet ownership was one of the best predictors of survival for patients with heart disease.[3]

Kay Miller, a chaplain and a licensed dog handler, gives a provocative case study from one of her pastoral care visits to a patient experiencing difficulty in communication with humans:

> While Mr. J was in the hospital to have his shoulder repaired, his wife died unexpectedly. He refused to discuss her death with family members or staff. They had a long happy marriage, and their three children were grown and married. When the children tried to talk about their mother and her death, Mr. J informed them that he did not want them to wait until his discharge for the funeral arrangements and burial, and said that he would discuss nothing more about her. He refused to reminisce, to express any emotion, or to allow those around him to express their emotions. He insisted, 'I refuse to deal with any of that now. I will handle it when I get home. Now talk about something else."
>
> The children were very frustrated with him—saying this just wasn't him, that he normally shared his feelings rather freely. Hospital chaplains as well as the family's religious leaders and a psychologist all visited with Mr. J. In each of these cases, his response was the same as it had been with his children. It was simply *not* a topic for conversation. He was always very pleasant and very willing to discuss any subject except his wife or death in general. 'I'll deal with that when I get home!' was his only response.
>
> Knowing that he owned a dog, we decided to try our Pastoral Care Dog, Scruffy. Arriving at his door, I said, 'Mr J, I thought you might like to see my dog.' He responded, 'Ah, poochie, come here to Papa!' Almost immediately, he became totally focused on Scruffy, seemingly unaware of my presence even though I sat on a chair about two feet to his side and in front of him.
>
> He began by telling Scruffy about his own dog and then progressed to stories about things he and his wife had done with their dog. Soon he was telling Scruffy about his wife, the things they had done together, and

how very much she meant to him. As he talked to Scruffy, she responded appropriately by resting her head on his leg, looking up at him, licking his hand, and nuzzling into the crook of his arm. The conversation had taken nearly an hour by this point. He had laughed, cried, and smiled. Scruffy seemed to be feeling with him. Then he said, 'That's why I have to do it, old boy, I just can't go on without her.' At this, Scruffy pulled away from him and gave him what appeared to be a very disapproving look. He reached for her, but she wouldn't budge.

Finally, he softened and said, 'You're right, old boy. I can't do it. Any way, if I did, she'd make heaven a living hell for me. I've got to stick around down here for a while more. It's just not my time yet.' As he said this, Scruffy nuzzled back into his lap. He went on to tell her about the things he was going to do with his grandchildren, planning a fishing trip with them as he talked about how much they still needed him and of his influence on them. Occasionally, he chuckled and said that his wife really would approve of all these things.

After another half hour, he seemed startled, and even frightened, as he said 'But I can't go on and do these things without you, old boy!' Finally, I spoke, and I reminded him that his own dog waited for him at home, and that this dog knew and loved his wife so he should be an even better listener that Scruffy had been. After all, Scruffy had never had the opportunity to meet his wife. He laughed and agreed, thanking me and hugging Scruffy.[4]

Chaplain Miller's study gave several case histories like the one above supporting the thesis that animals "can serve as a communication bridge for people when normal communication has been disrupted."[5] Furthermore, her study produced additional benefits because of the dog's presence which are as follows:

> The patient's family members and visitors expressed appreciation and seemed comforted. Informal visits

with those in the hospital waiting rooms provided distractions as well as soothing comfort. Employee morale appeared to be greatly improved when the dog was in the area. They seemed more understanding of each other and more available to respond happily to patient needs. 'Come over here. I need my doggie fix for the day' was often heard.[6]

In a large Australian study of animals and cardiovascular health, Gregory L. R. Jennings, Christopher M. Reid, Irene Christy, et al reported:

> Cardiovascular risk factors were examined in 5,741 healthy participants attending a screening service. Pet owners had significantly lower systolic blood pressure and plasma triglycerides than non-owners. There were significantly lower cholesterol values in men but not in women.[7]

This group also reported on the 1994 Australian People and Pet Survey, which included an actual calculation of money saved through fewer doctor visits, hospitalizations, and use of pharmaceuticals as a result of pet ownership.[8] Apparently, many people feel comfortable and receive benefit from communicating with animals.

Even more important, perhaps, is the emotional effect pets have on humans:

> When people face real adversity—disease, unemployment, or the disabilities of age—affection from a pet takes on a new meaning. Then the pet's continuing affection is a sign that the essence of the person has not been damaged.[9]

Sometime ago, I saw a bumper sticker that said: "Lord, help me be the person my dog thinks I am." Pets are spiritual and can teach us many spiritual lessons that can make us a better person. I have found this to be true in my personal experience and apparently many others have as well.

APPENDIX F
ACTIONS YOU CAN TAKE IN WORKING THROUGH YOUR SHAME

- Look for the feeling and needs underneath the shame. Shame is a cover-up.
- Shame needs to be acknowledged in intimate relationships as soon as it is recognized.
- Change your "should," "oughtas," "gottas," and "have tos," to "I choose to . . ." or "I choose not to . . ."
- Talk about it in supportive places. Go public (therapy, support groups, friends).
- Use your need for approval in a positive way. "Stick with the winners".
- Make friends with your shadow side, that is the drives, experiences, images, feelings and fantasies that were repressed during the course of your individual development.
- Find and process the unresolved issues of your past, most often found in your family of origin: the roots of shame.
- Deal with your loyalty to your family of origin. Refusal to do this is the single most hindering issue in recovery from shame.
- Learn to receive from others, especially compliments.
- Have compassion for yourself and patience with yourself.
- Seek out, nurture and love the child within you.

- Learn to replace your self-critical and self-abusive inner dialogue with affirmations and compassion.
- Accept your acceptance, that is accept the fact that God loves you and accepts you <u>just as you are.</u>
- If all the above fails seek therapy.

All of the above need to be done again and again. Shame is only overcome by interaction over a long period of time in ongoing, intimate relationships. If all the above fails see a therapist.

Author Unknown

REFERENCES

Introduction

1. Miller, Madeleine S and Miller, J. Lane. (1952). Harper's Bible Dictionary. New York: Harper & Brothers. p. 686.
2. Elkins, David N. (1999). Spirituality: It's What's Missing In Mental Health. Psychology Today, p. 45.
3. Grossman, Cathy Lynn. (2012). Protestants lose majority status in U.S. USA Today, p. 1.
4. Peck, M. Scott. (1978). The Road Less Traveled. New York: Simon & Schuster. p. 206.
5. Peck, p. 197.
6. Peck, p. 210.
7. Maslow, A. H. (1970). Religions, Values, and Peak-Experiences. New York: Penquin Books. p. 45.

Chapter 1: Spirituality and Religion

1. Maslow, A. H. (1970). Religions, Values and Peak-Experiences. New York: Penquin Books. p viii.
2. Elkins, David N. (1999). Spirituality: It's What's Missing In Mental Health. Psychology Today, p.47.
3. Pargament, Kenneth I. (2007). Spiritual Integrated Psychotherapy. New York: The Guilford Press. p. 2.

4. Peck, M. Scott. 1978. The Road Less Traveled. New York: Simon & Schuster. 2006. p.15
5. Frankl, Viktor E. (1959). Man's Search For Meaning. New York: Simon & Schuster. p. 3.
6. Frankl, p.84.
7. Clinebell, Howard. (1979). Growth Counseling. Nashville: Abingdon. p. 101.
8. Clinebell. p. 106.

Chapter 2: Seeking a Relationship with a Caring God, Higher Power.

1. Powell, S.J., John. (1975). A Reason to Live, a Reason to Die. Allen Texas: Argus Communications. p. 103-104.
2. Lebedoff, David. (2009). Imagine There's No Heaven . . . No Hell. St. Paul: Star Tribune. Com/Opinion. p. 1.
3. Peck, M. Scott. (1978). The Road Less Traveled. New York: Simon & Schuster. 2006. p. 190.
4. Roth, Lillian. (1953). I'll Cry Tomorrow. New York: Frederick Fell, Inc. p. 396.
5. Peck. p. 194
6. Powell, S.J., John. (1978). Unconditional Love. Allen Texas: Argus Communications p. 110-118.

Chapter 3: Living a Positive Philosophy of Life.

1. Park, Alice. (2009). Study: Optimistic Women Live Longer. Time: On Line Journal. p. 1.
2. Seligman, E.P., Martin: (1995). The Optimistic Child: A Proven Program to Safeguard Children Against Depression and Build Lifelong Resilience. New York: Houghton Mifflin Co. p. 115.
3. Seligman, p. 52.
4. Seligman, p. 52.
5. Seligman, p. 53.
6. Seligman, p. 52.
7. Seligman, p. 57.

8. Seligman, p. 57.
9. Seligman, p. 62.
10. Seligman, p. 51.
11. Seligman, p. 62.
12. Seligman, p. 53.

Chapter 4: Overcoming Shame

1. Middleton-Moz, Jane. (1990). Shame & Guilt: The Masters of Disguise. Florida: Health Communications, Inc. p. xii-xiii.

Chapter 5: Renewing Moments of Transcendence.

1. Maslow, A. H. (1990). Religions, Values, and Peak Experiences. New York: Penquin Books. p. xvi.
2. Maslow, A. H. (1971). The Farther Reaches of Human Nature. New York: Viking Press. p. 105.
3. Maslow, p. xiv.
4. Maslow, p. xv.
5. Newberg, Andrew. Waldman, Mark R. (2009). How God Changes Your Brain. New York: Ballantine Books. p. 35.

Chapter 6: Being Congruent With Our Values

1. Maslow, A. H. (1968). Toward a Psychology of Being. New York: Van Nostrand: pp. xx, Nostrand. pp. xx, iv, 206.
2. Clinebell, Howard. (1979) Growth Counseling. Nashville: Abingdon. p. 118.
3. Clinebell, p. 118.
4. Alcoholics Anonymous: Third Edition. (1976). The Big Book. Alcoholics Anonymous World Services, Inc. New York City: New York. p. 58.

Chapter 7. Trusting and Being Trusted

1. Johnson, Vernon. (1980). I'll Quit Tomorrow. New York: Harper and Row. rev. ed. p. 124.
2. Woodruff, Sue. (1982). Meditations With Mechtild of Magdeburg. New Mexico: Bear and Company, Inc. p. 69.
3. Spring, Janis. A. (2004). How Can I Forgive You. New York: Harper-Collins. p. 47.
4. Freeman, Criswell. Dr. (2006). Friends Are Forever. New York: Simon and Schuster, Inc. p. 47.

Chapter 8. Joining Caring and Nurturing Communities

1. Clinebell, Howard. (1979). Growth Counseling. Nashville: Abingdon Press. pps. 125-126.
2. Maslow, A. H. (1990). Religions, Values, and Peak Experiences. New York: Penquin Books, p. xiii.
3. Peck, M. Scott. (1978). The Road Less Traveled. New York: Simon and Schuster, p.194.
4. Obiesesan, T. Livingstone I, Trulear HD, Gillum F. Frequency of attendance at religious services, cardiovascular disease, metabolic risk factors and dietary intake in Americans: age-stratafied exploratory analysis. Int J Psychiatry Med. 2006; 36(4): 435-48.
5. Tanner, Ira J. (1973). The Fear of Love. New York: Harper and Row, p. 22.
6. Kennedy, Eugene. (1976). The Joy of Being Human. New York: Doubleday, p. 321.

Chapter 9: Developing Our Higher Self

1. Clinebell, Howard. (1979). Growth Counseling. Nashville: Abingdon. p. 123.
2. Kennedy, Eugene. (1976). The Joy of Being Human. New York: Doubleday. p. 322.

3. Buechner, Frederick. (1991). The Sacred Journey. San Francisco: Harper Collins Publisher, p. 7.

APPENDIX D

1. Beck, Alan and Katcher, Aaron. (1996). Between Pets and People—The Importance of Animal Companionship. Indiana: University Press, p. 94.
2. Ibid., p. 14.
3. Ibid., p. 3-5.
4. Miller, Kay. *Making the Rounds with the Pastoral Care Dog*. Chaplaincy Today. Vol. 17, Number 2. Winter 2001.
5. Ibid., p. 27.
6. Ibid., p. 27.
7. Jennings, Gregory L. R., Reid, Christopher M., Christy, Irene, et al, (1998). "Animals and Cardiovascular Health." *Companion Animals in Human Health*. Thousand Oaks, CA: Sage Publications, 161.
8. Ibid., 169.
9. Beck and Katcher, *Between Pets and People*, p. 29.

Printed in Germany
by Amazon Distribution
GmbH, Leipzig